Math Activities

This book belongs to

W9-AWC-008

FS109039 • Math Activities

Our Growing Garden

Find the sums. Color the plants with answers that are even.

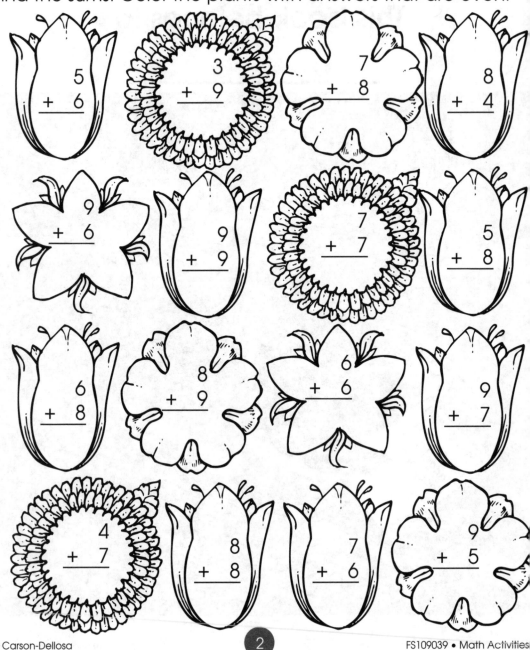

$$\begin{array}{r} 5 \\ +\ 6 \\ \hline \end{array}$$

$$\begin{array}{r} 3 \\ +\ 9 \\ \hline \end{array}$$

$$\begin{array}{r} 7 \\ +\ 8 \\ \hline \end{array}$$

$$\begin{array}{r} 8 \\ +\ 4 \\ \hline \end{array}$$

$$\begin{array}{r} 9 \\ +\ 6 \\ \hline \end{array}$$

$$\begin{array}{r} 9 \\ +\ 9 \\ \hline \end{array}$$

$$\begin{array}{r} 7 \\ +\ 7 \\ \hline \end{array}$$

$$\begin{array}{r} 5 \\ +\ 8 \\ \hline \end{array}$$

$$\begin{array}{r} 6 \\ +\ 8 \\ \hline \end{array}$$

$$\begin{array}{r} 8 \\ +\ 9 \\ \hline \end{array}$$

$$\begin{array}{r} 6 \\ +\ 6 \\ \hline \end{array}$$

$$\begin{array}{r} 9 \\ +\ 7 \\ \hline \end{array}$$

$$\begin{array}{r} 4 \\ +\ 7 \\ \hline \end{array}$$

$$\begin{array}{r} 8 \\ +\ 8 \\ \hline \end{array}$$

$$\begin{array}{r} 7 \\ +\ 6 \\ \hline \end{array}$$

$$\begin{array}{r} 9 \\ +\ 5 \\ \hline \end{array}$$

FS109039 • Math Activities

Who Will Be First?

Find the sums one at a time from left to right. After each sum, move an insect toward the center of the flower by coloring the petal with the matching number. Circle the bug that reaches the center.

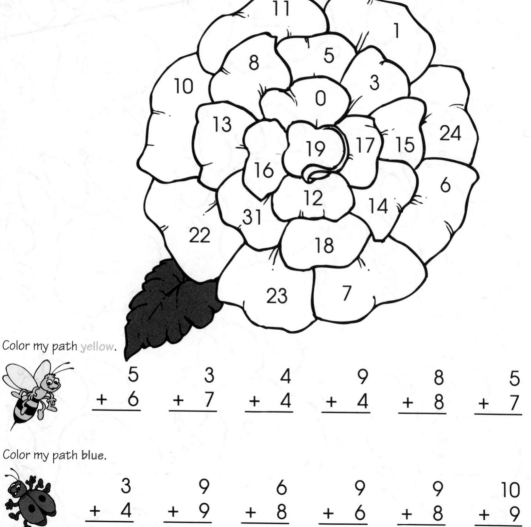

Color my path yellow.

$$\begin{array}{r} 5 \\ + 6 \\ \hline \end{array} \qquad \begin{array}{r} 3 \\ + 7 \\ \hline \end{array} \qquad \begin{array}{r} 4 \\ + 4 \\ \hline \end{array} \qquad \begin{array}{r} 9 \\ + 4 \\ \hline \end{array} \qquad \begin{array}{r} 8 \\ + 8 \\ \hline \end{array} \qquad \begin{array}{r} 5 \\ + 7 \\ \hline \end{array}$$

Color my path blue.

$$\begin{array}{r} 3 \\ + 4 \\ \hline \end{array} \qquad \begin{array}{r} 9 \\ + 9 \\ \hline \end{array} \qquad \begin{array}{r} 6 \\ + 8 \\ \hline \end{array} \qquad \begin{array}{r} 9 \\ + 6 \\ \hline \end{array} \qquad \begin{array}{r} 9 \\ + 8 \\ \hline \end{array} \qquad \begin{array}{r} 10 \\ + 9 \\ \hline \end{array}$$

FS109039 • Math Activities

Paw Prints

Find the differences.

$$\begin{array}{r} 12 \\ -\ 6 \\ \hline \end{array}$$

$$\begin{array}{r} 11 \\ -\ 4 \\ \hline \end{array}$$

$$\begin{array}{r} 15 \\ -\ 9 \\ \hline \end{array}$$

$$\begin{array}{r} 13 \\ -\ 9 \\ \hline \end{array}$$

$$\begin{array}{r} 14 \\ -\ 8 \\ \hline \end{array}$$

$$\begin{array}{r} 11 \\ -\ 5 \\ \hline \end{array}$$

$$\begin{array}{r} 14 \\ -\ 7 \\ \hline \end{array}$$

$$\begin{array}{r} 16 \\ -\ 9 \\ \hline \end{array}$$

$$\begin{array}{r} 16 \\ -\ 8 \\ \hline \end{array}$$

4

FS109039 • Math Activities

In the Doghouse!

Find the differences. Color the bones with answers that are odd numbers to help Dugan get back to her house.

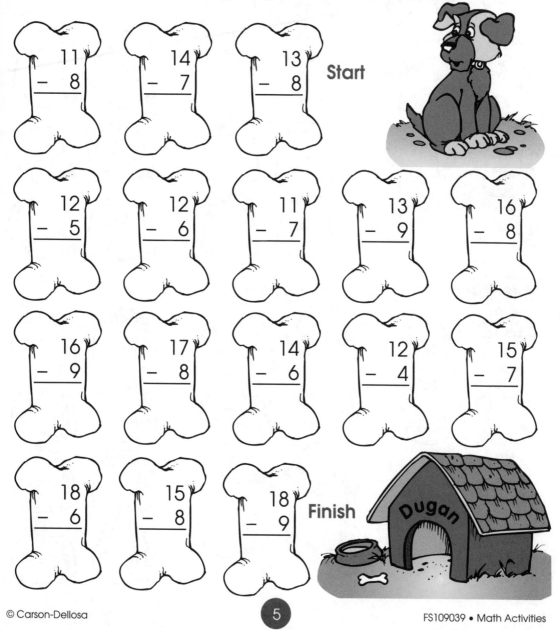

$\begin{array}{r} 11 \\ -\ 8 \\ \hline \end{array}$

$\begin{array}{r} 14 \\ -\ 7 \\ \hline \end{array}$

$\begin{array}{r} 13 \\ -\ 8 \\ \hline \end{array}$ **Start**

$\begin{array}{r} 12 \\ -\ 5 \\ \hline \end{array}$

$\begin{array}{r} 12 \\ -\ 6 \\ \hline \end{array}$

$\begin{array}{r} 11 \\ -\ 7 \\ \hline \end{array}$

$\begin{array}{r} 13 \\ -\ 9 \\ \hline \end{array}$

$\begin{array}{r} 16 \\ -\ 8 \\ \hline \end{array}$

$\begin{array}{r} 16 \\ -\ 9 \\ \hline \end{array}$

$\begin{array}{r} 17 \\ -\ 8 \\ \hline \end{array}$

$\begin{array}{r} 14 \\ -\ 6 \\ \hline \end{array}$

$\begin{array}{r} 12 \\ -\ 4 \\ \hline \end{array}$

$\begin{array}{r} 15 \\ -\ 7 \\ \hline \end{array}$

$\begin{array}{r} 18 \\ -\ 6 \\ \hline \end{array}$

$\begin{array}{r} 15 \\ -\ 8 \\ \hline \end{array}$

$\begin{array}{r} 18 \\ -\ 9 \\ \hline \end{array}$ **Finish**

Dugan

All Dressed Up

Write the number that comes next.

 23

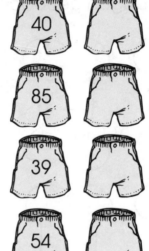 40

 19

76

85

61

97

39

92

58

54

70

Write the number that comes before.

 92

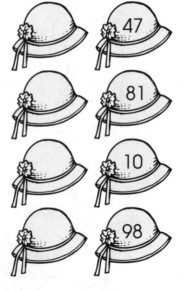 47

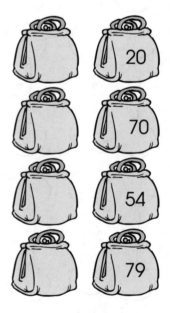 20

33

81

70

65

10

54

86

98

79

FS109039 • Math Activities

Clotheslines

Write the missing numbers.

    FS109039 • Math Activities

Double Digits

Write how many tens and ones. Write the numbers as an addition problem. Then, write the sum.

___3___ tens ___5___ ones

___30___ + ___5___

___35___

_____ tens _____ ones

_____ + _____

_____

_____ tens _____ ones

_____ + _____

_____

_____ tens _____ ones

_____ + _____

_____

_____ tens _____ ones

_____ + _____

_____

_____ tens _____ ones

_____ + _____

_____

Which Vegetable Is It?

Use the clues to answer each riddle.

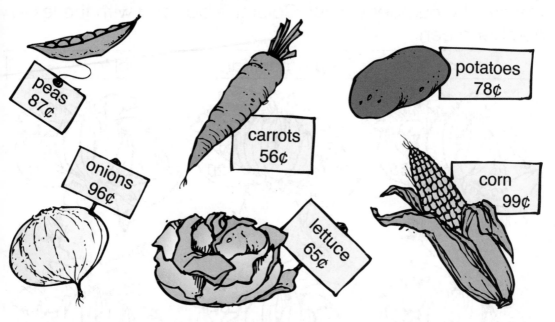

1. We cost 70¢ and 8¢. What are we? _____

2. We cost 8 tens and 7 ones. What are we? _____

3. We cost between 55¢ and 57¢. What are we? _____

4. We cost 90¢ and 6¢. What are we? _____

5. Our price is the highest two-digit number. What are we?

    _____

6. We cost 5 ones and 6 tens. What are we? _____

FS109039 • Math Activities

Go Bananas!

Write <, >, or = on each tree trunk. Color the banana with the greater number yellow. Color the banana with the lesser number green.

| < less than | > greater than | = equal to |

FS109039 • Math Activities

Jungle Hunt

Help the monkey get to the bananas by coloring a path of connecting leaves. Start at 0 and color the leaves in order from least to greatest.

63 55 40 51

90 80

31 29

17 62

0 68

81 50

4 22 81

1 77 45

11 38 8 89

47

56 96

21 23 25

56 15 78

FS109039 • Math Activities

The Early Bird

Write the time above each worm.

Draw the hands on the clocks to show the given times.

Nesting Time

Write the time on each nest.

Draw the hands on the clocks to show the given times.

5:50

1:25

9:55

1:05

Take a Hike!

Complete the path by following the directions on the stones.
Draw the hands to show the new times.

Start

One hour later

Two hours earlier

Six hours later

Four hours later

One hour earlier

Finish

Two hours earlier

Four hours later

14

FS109039 • Math Activities

A Day at Camp

Write the time at which each camper finished his or her activity.

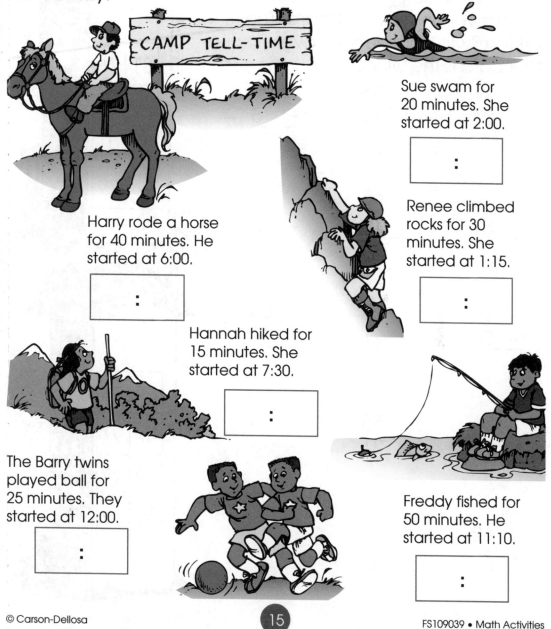

CAMP TELL-TIME

Sue swam for 20 minutes. She started at 2:00.

Harry rode a horse for 40 minutes. He started at 6:00.

Renee climbed rocks for 30 minutes. She started at 1:15.

Hannah hiked for 15 minutes. She started at 7:30.

The Barry twins played ball for 25 minutes. They started at 12:00.

Freddy fished for 50 minutes. He started at 11:10.

15

FS109039 • Math Activities

Family Feud

Who will win? Find each sum
working from left to right. Shade
the answer on a bingo board. The
first family to completely cover
their card is the winner!

81	76
49	35
74	91
98	79

```
    11          36          90
 + 24        + 33         +  8


    25          87          36
 + 51        + 12         +  3


    29          28          80
 + 50        + 21         + 11


    36          55          16
 + 11        + 31         + 13


    62          43          41
 + 35        + 31         + 15
```

69	56
47	97
99	29
86	39

FS109039 • Math Activities

What's Missing?

Fill in the missing numbers to make the problems work.

$$\begin{array}{r} 3\ \square \\ +\ \square\ \ 2 \\ \hline 9\ \ 5 \end{array}$$

$$\begin{array}{r} 2\ \ 4 \\ +\ \square\ \square \\ \hline 6\ \ 6 \end{array}$$

$$\begin{array}{r} 5\ \square \\ +\ 2\ \ 4 \\ \hline \square\ \ 6 \end{array}$$

$$\begin{array}{r} \square\ \ 1 \\ +\ 5\ \square \\ \hline 8\ \ 3 \end{array}$$

$$\begin{array}{r} \square\ \ 3 \\ +\ 1\ \ 4 \\ \hline 7\ \square \end{array}$$

$$\begin{array}{r} 5\ \ 3 \\ +\ 4\ \ 6 \\ \hline \square\ \square \end{array}$$

$$\begin{array}{r} 2\ \square \\ +\ \square\ \ 3 \\ \hline 9\ \ 6 \end{array}$$

$$\begin{array}{r} 5\ \ 3 \\ +\ \square\ \square \\ \hline 7\ \ 8 \end{array}$$

$$\begin{array}{r} 8\ \square \\ +\ 1\ \ 2 \\ \hline \square\ \ 7 \end{array}$$

$$\begin{array}{r} \square\ \ 0 \\ +\ 4\ \square \\ \hline 5\ \ 8 \end{array}$$

$$\begin{array}{r} \square\ \ 3 \\ +\ 6\ \ 2 \\ \hline 7\ \square \end{array}$$

$$\begin{array}{r} 5\ \ 4 \\ +\ 3\ \ 5 \\ \hline \square\ \square \end{array}$$

Banners High

Find the sums by regrouping. Then, color the flags by their sums.

20 to 39 purple	40 to 59 yellow	60 to 79 red	80 to 99 blue

$$58 + 13$$

$$23 + 17$$

$$64 + 29$$

$$15 + 15$$

$$44 + 9$$

$$57 + 37$$

$$27 + 6$$

$$46 + 28$$

$$45 + 49$$

$$18 + 19$$

$$38 + 38$$

$$36 + 16$$

FS109039 • Math Activities

Fourth of July

Answer each problem by regrouping. Use the sums to answer the riddle.

Where was the Declaration of Independence signed?

$\overline{35}$ $\overline{70}$ $\overline{70}$ $\overline{94}$ $\overline{88}$ $\overline{61}$ $\overline{83}$ $\overline{70}$ $\overline{70}$ $\overline{83}$ $\overline{91}$!

R	O	L	B	P
63 + 29	54 + 29	63 + 27	35 + 26	46 + 17

H	C	A	K	M
76 + 18	38 + 38	18 + 17	24 + 38	82 + 9

S	I	N	T	E
15 + 27	39 + 15	18 + 29	46 + 24	49 + 39

FS109039 • Math Activities

The Ball Game

Which team will win? Find each difference, working from left to right. Shade the answer on a bingo board. The first team to completely cover its card is the winner!

SCOREBOARD

FASTBACKS

46	22	59	71
73	68	35	43

SWANS

21	34	62	32
51	78	23	30

$$
\begin{array}{r} 96 \\ -\ 25 \\ \hline \end{array}
\qquad
\begin{array}{r} 43 \\ -\ 20 \\ \hline \end{array}
\qquad
\begin{array}{r} 65 \\ -\ 44 \\ \hline \end{array}
\qquad
\begin{array}{r} 98 \\ -\ 63 \\ \hline \end{array}
\qquad
\begin{array}{r} 74 \\ -\ 52 \\ \hline \end{array}
$$

$$
\begin{array}{r} 81 \\ -\ 51 \\ \hline \end{array}
\qquad
\begin{array}{r} 57 \\ -\ 23 \\ \hline \end{array}
\qquad
\begin{array}{r} 66 \\ -\ 34 \\ \hline \end{array}
\qquad
\begin{array}{r} 89 \\ -\ 16 \\ \hline \end{array}
\qquad
\begin{array}{r} 68 \\ -\ 25 \\ \hline \end{array}
$$

$$
\begin{array}{r} 99 \\ -\ 48 \\ \hline \end{array}
\qquad
\begin{array}{r} 98 \\ -\ 36 \\ \hline \end{array}
\qquad
\begin{array}{r} 79 \\ -\ 20 \\ \hline \end{array}
\qquad
\begin{array}{r} 88 \\ -\ 42 \\ \hline \end{array}
\qquad
\begin{array}{r} 99 \\ -\ 31 \\ \hline \end{array}
$$

Batter Up!

Rename each number by regrouping. Take from the tens place and give to the ones place as shown.

36 = 3 tens and 6 ones = __2__ tens and __16__ ones

72 = 7 tens and 2 ones = _____ tens and _____ ones

50 = 5 tens and 0 ones = _____ tens and _____ ones

23 = 2 tens and 3 ones = _____ tens and _____ ones

85 = 8 tens and 5 ones = _____ tens and _____ ones

90 = 9 tens and 0 ones = _____ tens and _____ ones

64 = 6 tens and 4 ones = _____ tens and _____ ones

Uh-Oh!

Answer each problem by regrouping. Use the differences to answer the riddle.

Why didn't the mountain climber yell for help?

$\overline{35}$ $\overline{28}$ $\overline{9}$ $\overline{67}$ $\overline{63}$

$\overline{35}$ $\overline{67}$ $\overline{25}$ $\overline{46}$ $\overline{52}$ $\overline{25}$ $\overline{46}$

$\overline{17}$ $\overline{74}$ $\overline{35}$ $\overline{52}$ $\overline{63}$

$\overline{19}$ $\overline{28}$ $\overline{28}$ $\overline{19}$ $\overline{35}$ **!**

G $\begin{array}{r} 62 \\ - 16 \end{array}$	T $\begin{array}{r} 48 \\ - 29 \end{array}$	R $\begin{array}{r} 83 \\ - 34 \end{array}$	W $\begin{array}{r} 91 \\ - 82 \end{array}$	E $\begin{array}{r} 56 \\ - 28 \end{array}$
A $\begin{array}{r} 74 \\ - 7 \end{array}$	D $\begin{array}{r} 57 \\ - 19 \end{array}$	H $\begin{array}{r} 64 \\ - 29 \end{array}$	Y $\begin{array}{r} 92 \\ - 18 \end{array}$	I $\begin{array}{r} 81 \\ - 29 \end{array}$
B $\begin{array}{r} 36 \\ - 19 \end{array}$	S $\begin{array}{r} 71 \\ - 8 \end{array}$	F $\begin{array}{r} 54 \\ - 49 \end{array}$	N $\begin{array}{r} 43 \\ - 18 \end{array}$	C $\begin{array}{r} 87 \\ - 48 \end{array}$

Down the Slope!

Find the differences. The number in the snowflakes will answer the question.

Mount McKinley is the tallest mountain in North America. How high is it?

$$\begin{array}{r} 96 \\ -\ 25 \\ \hline \square \end{array}$$

$$\begin{array}{r} -\ 18 \\ \hline \square \end{array}$$

$$\begin{array}{r} 82 \\ -\ 16 \\ \hline \square \end{array}$$

$$\begin{array}{r} -\ 29 \\ \hline \square \end{array}$$

$$\begin{array}{r} -\ 36 \\ \hline \square \end{array}$$

$$\begin{array}{r} 76 \\ -\ 38 \\ \hline \square \end{array}$$

$$\begin{array}{r} -\ 18 \\ \hline \end{array}$$

$$\begin{array}{r} -\ 29 \\ \hline \end{array}$$

$$\begin{array}{r} -\ 29 \\ \hline \end{array}$$

$$\begin{array}{r} 80 \\ -\ 76 \\ \hline \end{array}$$

Mount McKinley is ____, ____ ____ ____ meters high!

The Souvenir Shop

Count the coins to find the cost of each souvenir. Write the price on the tag.

Washington Monument

Liberty Bell

St. Louis Gateway Arch

Yellowstone Park

Niagara Falls

Seattle Space Needle

FS109039 • Math Activities

Shopping for Souvenirs

Color the coins needed to make exact change for each item.

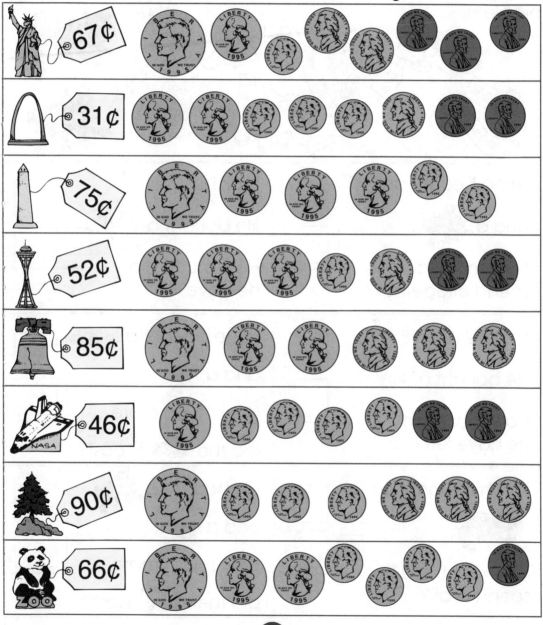

Buy Beanbag Babies

Use the prices of the toy animals to write and solve each problem.

Anna bought a 🐛 and a 🐊 . How much did she spend altogether?

Nick had 92¢ He bought a 🦘 . How much did he have left?

Stephen had 84¢ He bought a 🐷 . How much did he have left?

Rosie bought a 🐱 and a 🐰 . How much more did the 🐱 cost?

Mitch bought two 🦝 . How much did he spend in all?

Lily bought a 🐸 and a 🐛 . How much more did the 🐸 cost?

FS109039 • Math Activities

Which Baby Is It?

Use the toys and price tags from page 26 to find prices and complete the puzzle.

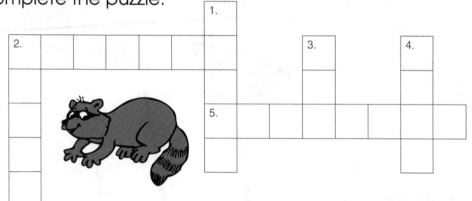

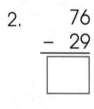

Across

2.
```
   76
 - 29
 ____
```

5.
```
   46
 + 27
 ____
```

6.
```
   84
 - 27
 ____
```

Word Bank

rabbit	kangaroo	raccoon
frog	pig	snake	tiger

Down

1.
```
   52
 - 26
 ____
```

2.
```
   78
 - 39
 ____
```

3.
```
   19
 + 19
 ____
```

4.
```
   25
 + 15
 ____
```

Space Invasion

Measure the length of the path from each spaceship to Earth. Write the length in centimeters (cm) on each line.

The Space of a Spaceship

Measure the length of each line with a centimeter ruler. Then, add to find the distance around each spaceship (perimeter).

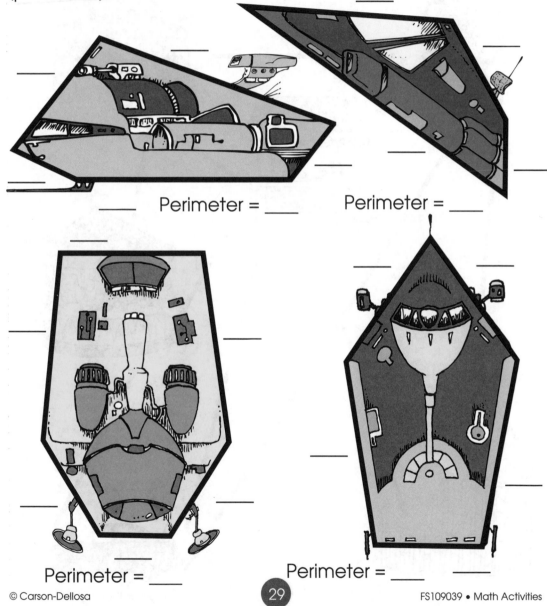

Perimeter = ___

Perimeter = ___

Perimeter = ___

Perimeter = ___

FS109039 • Math Activities

Fairgrounds

Measure each line with an inch ruler. Write the measurements by the lines.

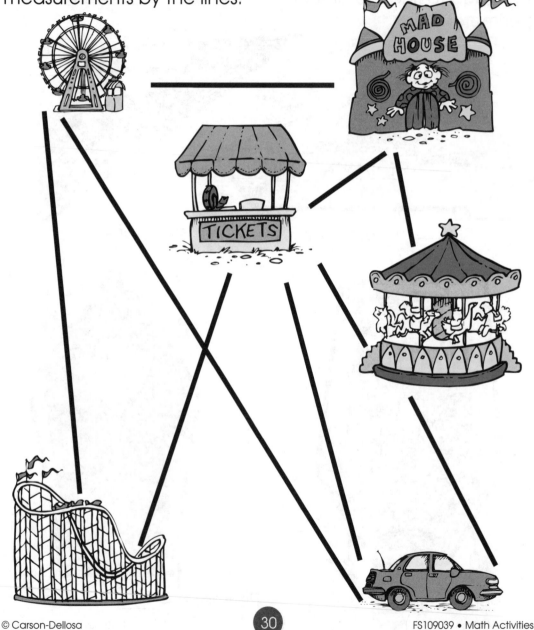

Fun at the Fair

The lists show where the kids walked at the fair. Use the measurements from page 30 to find the total distances they walked.

Trey's Trip

Start at

Then to ☐

Then to ☐

Then to ☐

Then to ☐

Last to ☐

How far was Trey's trip at the fair? _____

Jenny's Journey

Start at

Then to ☐

Then to ☐

Then to ☐

Then to ☐

Last to ☐

How far was Jenny's journey at the fair? _____

FS109039 • Math Activities

Fishing Around

Write how many hundreds (h), tens (t), and ones (o). Then, write the three-digit number.

__ h __ t __ o

_____

__ h __ t __ o

_____

__ h __ t __ o

_____

__ h __ t __ o

_____

__ h __ t __ o

_____

© Carson-Dellosa   FS109039 • Math Activities

Under the Sea

Count the money. Write the number of hundreds (h), tens (t), and ones (o). Write the three-digit number, using the dollar sign ($) and decimal point (.).

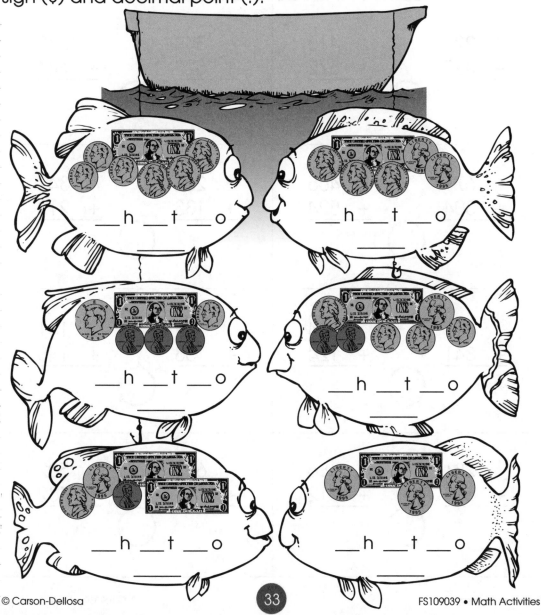

__ h __ t __ o

_____

__ h __ t __ o

_____

__ h __ t __ o

_____

__ h __ t __ o

_____

__ h __ t __ o

_____

__ h __ t __ o

_____

FS109039 • Math Activities

Add It Up

Find the sums. Write >, <, or = in the circles to compare the sums.

221 + 425	◯	416 + 572	344 + 523	◯	243 + 444

221
+ 425   ◯   416
+ 572

344
+ 523   ◯   243
+ 444

671
+ 304   ◯   465
+ 524

206
+ 133   ◯   347
+ 212

417
+ 341   ◯   634
+ 124

142
+ 153   ◯   141
+ 148

281
+ 612   ◯   386
+ 312

623
+ 311   ◯   502
+ 432

FS109039 • Math Activities

Let's Go!

Add to find each sum. Be sure to regroup from the ones to the tens place. Then, find and circle the sums hidden in the puzzle.

345	374	175	517	632
+ 429	+ 206	+ 416	+ 406	+ 328

446	385	705	618	617
+ 129	+ 107	+ 205	+ 345	+ 177

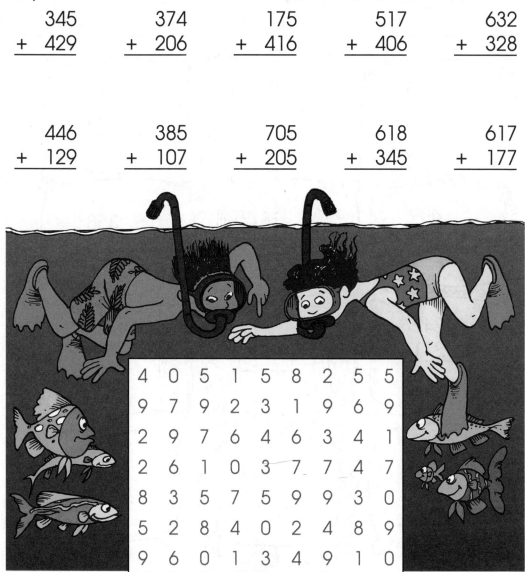

```
4 0 5 1 5 8 2 5 5
9 7 9 2 3 1 9 6 9
2 9 7 6 4 6 3 4 1
2 6 1 0 3 7 7 4 7
8 3 5 7 5 9 9 3 0
5 2 8 4 0 2 4 8 9
9 6 0 1 3 4 9 1 0
```

FS109039 • Math Activities

Sweet Dreams

Find each sum by regrouping from the tens to the hundreds place. Then, color the pillows.

0 to 199	200 to 399	400 to 599	600 to 799	800 to 999
blue	green	purple	red	orange

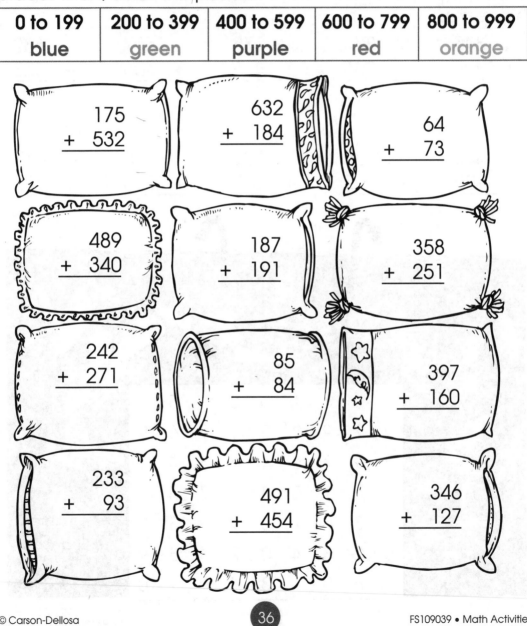

$$175 + 532$$

$$632 + 184$$

$$64 + 73$$

$$489 + 340$$

$$187 + 191$$

$$358 + 251$$

$$242 + 271$$

$$85 + 84$$

$$397 + 160$$

$$233 + 93$$

$$491 + 454$$

$$346 + 127$$

FS109039 • Math Activities

Counting Sheep

Add. Use the sums to answer the riddle.

Why did the sheep get a traffic ticket?

892	470	624

681	684	936	785	712	389

684		565	982	565

!

577	913	624	712

M 263 + 418	I 304 + 481	U 782 + 131	R 517 + 107	E 380 + 185
K 463 + 473	F 806 + 86	T 283 + 294	A 435 + 249	S 137 + 645
N 292 + 420	W 641 + 341	O 349 + 121	G 194 + 195	Y 111 + 222

© Carson-Dellosa

FS109039 • Math Activities

That Bugs Me!

Subtract. Then, color the squares with answers that are odd numbers to help the bug get to the leaf.

518 − 414	842 − 621	966 − 234	549 − 321
916 − 113	385 − 224	309 − 203	977 − 863
459 − 100	749 − 637	496 − 260	928 − 210
839 − 324	578 − 241	659 − 6	948 − 243

Big-Backed Bugs

Subtract. Be sure to regroup from the tens place to the ones place.

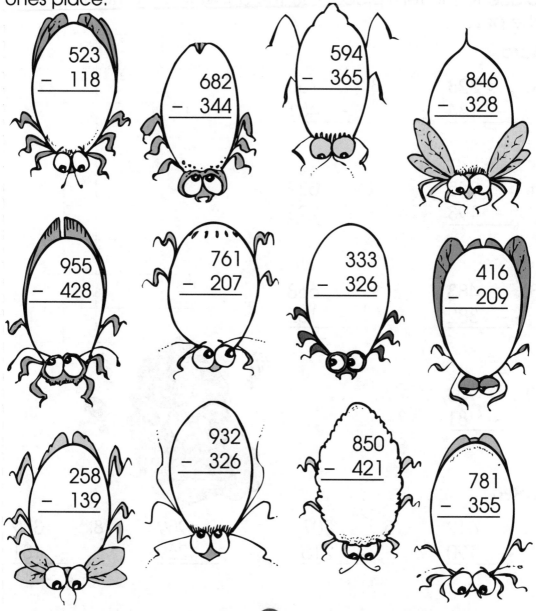

$$\begin{array}{r} 523 \\ -\ 118 \\ \hline \end{array}$$

$$\begin{array}{r} 682 \\ -\ 344 \\ \hline \end{array}$$

$$\begin{array}{r} 594 \\ -\ 365 \\ \hline \end{array}$$

$$\begin{array}{r} 846 \\ -\ 328 \\ \hline \end{array}$$

$$\begin{array}{r} 955 \\ -\ 428 \\ \hline \end{array}$$

$$\begin{array}{r} 761 \\ -\ 207 \\ \hline \end{array}$$

$$\begin{array}{r} 333 \\ -\ 326 \\ \hline \end{array}$$

$$\begin{array}{r} 416 \\ -\ 209 \\ \hline \end{array}$$

$$\begin{array}{r} 258 \\ -\ 139 \\ \hline \end{array}$$

$$\begin{array}{r} 932 \\ -\ 326 \\ \hline \end{array}$$

$$\begin{array}{r} 850 \\ -\ 421 \\ \hline \end{array}$$

$$\begin{array}{r} 781 \\ -\ 355 \\ \hline \end{array}$$

    FS109039 • Math Activities

That's Puzzling

Find each difference. Be sure to regroup from the hundreds place to the tens place. Use the answers to complete the puzzle.

Across

1.
$$\begin{array}{r} 328 \\ -\ 184 \\ \hline \end{array}$$

3.
$$\begin{array}{r} 735 \\ -\ 451 \\ \hline \end{array}$$

4.
$$\begin{array}{r} 945 \\ -\ 193 \\ \hline \end{array}$$

6.
$$\begin{array}{r} 589 \\ -\ 293 \\ \hline \end{array}$$

8.
$$\begin{array}{r} 483 \\ -\ 382 \\ \hline \end{array}$$

9.
$$\begin{array}{r} 668 \\ -\ 182 \\ \hline \end{array}$$

10.
$$\begin{array}{r} 903 \\ -\ 81 \\ \hline \end{array}$$

Down

2.
$$\begin{array}{r} 612 \\ -\ 190 \\ \hline \end{array}$$

5.
$$\begin{array}{r} 807 \\ -\ 215 \\ \hline \end{array}$$

7.
$$\begin{array}{r} 959 \\ -\ 269 \\ \hline \end{array}$$

8.
$$\begin{array}{r} 349 \\ -\ 181 \\ \hline \end{array}$$

    FS109039 • Math Activities

The Great Puzzle Race

Which team will put its puzzle together first? Find each difference, working from left to right. Shade the answer on the puzzle. The first team to completely cover its puzzle is the winner!

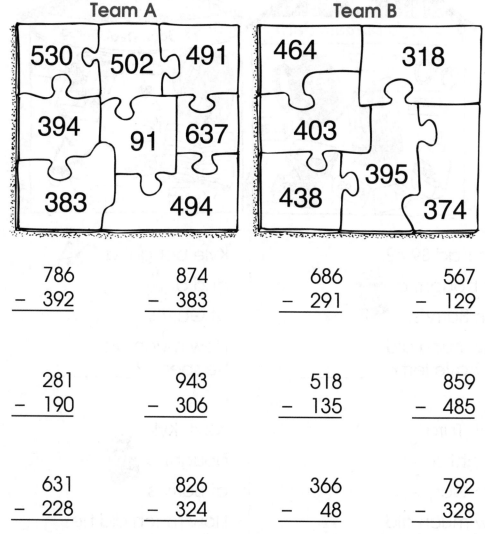

Team A

530	502	491
394	91	637
383		494

Team B

464		318
403		395
438		374

$$\begin{array}{r} 786 \\ -\ 392 \end{array}\qquad \begin{array}{r} 874 \\ -\ 383 \end{array}\qquad \begin{array}{r} 686 \\ -\ 291 \end{array}\qquad \begin{array}{r} 567 \\ -\ 129 \end{array}$$

$$\begin{array}{r} 281 \\ -\ 190 \end{array}\qquad \begin{array}{r} 943 \\ -\ 306 \end{array}\qquad \begin{array}{r} 518 \\ -\ 135 \end{array}\qquad \begin{array}{r} 859 \\ -\ 485 \end{array}$$

$$\begin{array}{r} 631 \\ -\ 228 \end{array}\qquad \begin{array}{r} 826 \\ -\ 324 \end{array}\qquad \begin{array}{r} 366 \\ -\ 48 \end{array}\qquad \begin{array}{r} 792 \\ -\ 328 \end{array}$$

Barry's or Gary's?

Use the prices below to write addition or subtraction problems. Then, find the answers.

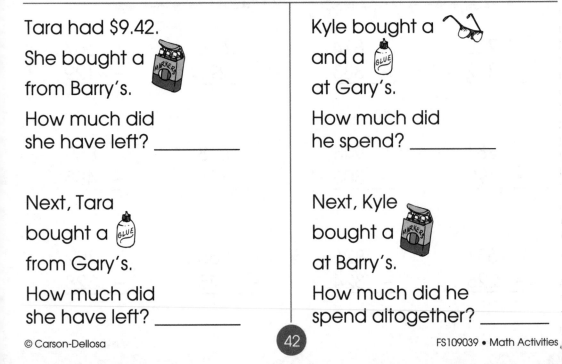

Tara had $9.42.

She bought a [markers] from Barry's.

How much did she have left? _____

Kyle bought a [glasses] and a [glue] at Gary's.

How much did he spend? _____

Next, Tara bought a [glue] from Gary's.

How much did she have left? _____

Next, Kyle bought a [markers] at Barry's.

How much did he spend altogether? _____

© Carson-Dellosa

FS109039 • Math Activities

More Barry's and Gary's

Read each story. Use the pictures and price tags on page 42 to find the prices. Write and solve an addition or subtraction problem.

Darcy shopped at Gary's.

She bought a 👓

and a [GLUE] .

How much did she spend in all?

Devin had $4.33.

He bought a 📓 at Barry's.

How much did he have left?

How much more

is a 📓 at

Barry's than at Gary's?

Brandon bought

two [MARKERS]

at Gary's.

How much did he spend altogether?

How much more

is a 🎒 at

Gary's than at Barry's?

Hannah had $7.81.

She bought a 🎒

at Barry's.

How much does she have left?

Home Sweet Home

Count the number of each kind of candy on the house.
Color one part of the graph for each candy you count.

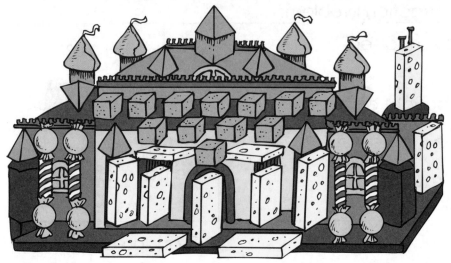

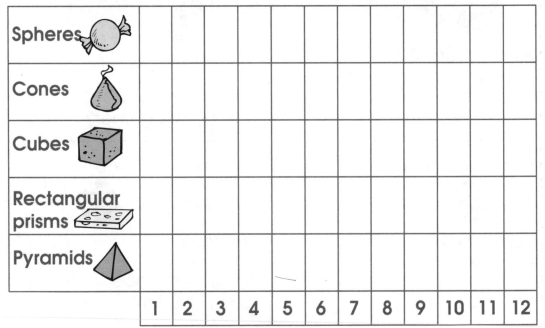

Spheres												
Cones												
Cubes												
Rectangular prisms												
Pyramids												
	1	2	3	4	5	6	7	8	9	10	11	12

FS109039 • Math Activities

More Home Sweet Home

Use the information from your graph on page 44 to write addition or subtraction problems. Then, find the answers.

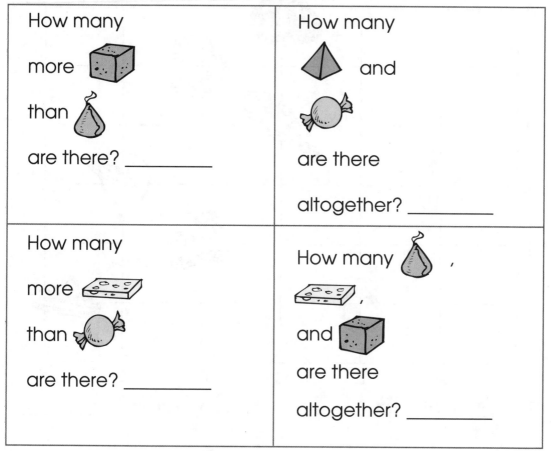

How many

more ⬜

than 🍬

are there? _____

How many

🔺 and

🍬

are there

altogether? _____

How many

more ▱

than 🍬

are there? _____

How many 🍬 ,

▱ ,

and 🟫

are there

altogether? _____

Which candy is used the least? _____

Which two candies total 17 pieces? _____

If the back of the house is exactly like the front, how many are there on the house altogether? _____

FS109039 • Math Activities

The Lost Treasure

Find the lost treasures. Write the letter and then the number as shown.

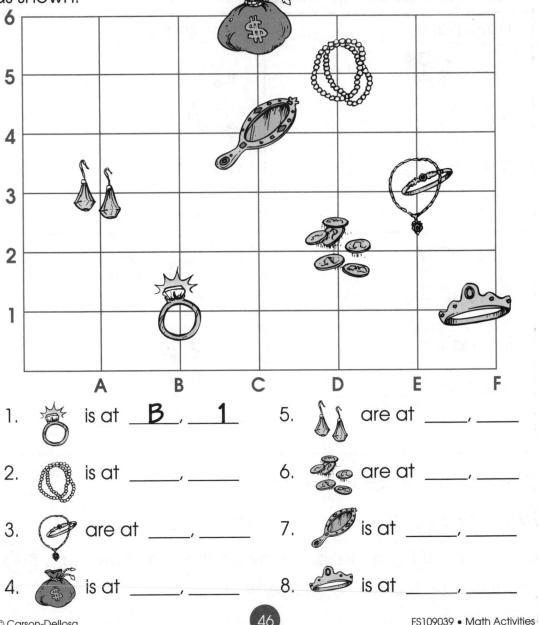

1. is at __B__, __1__

2. is at _____, _____

3. are at _____, _____

4. is at _____, _____

5. are at _____, _____

6. are at _____, _____

7. is at _____, _____

8. is at _____, _____

FS109039 • Math Activities

The Pirate Map

The pirates have hidden the treasure chest! Find the items by following the letters first and then the numbers. Write the name of each.

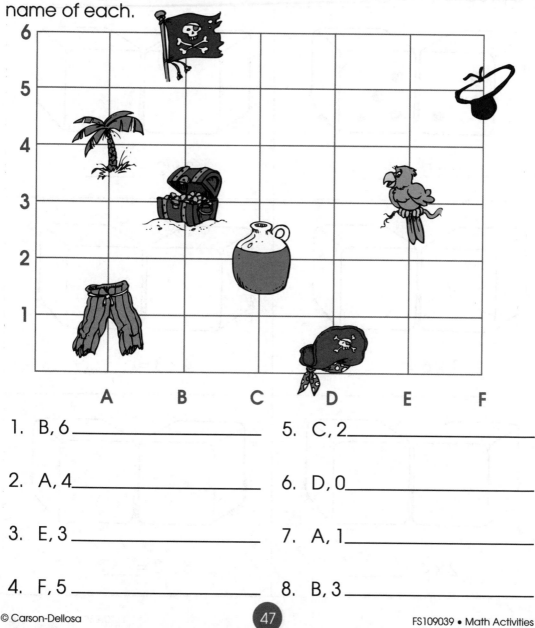

1. B, 6 _____

2. A, 4 _____

3. E, 3 _____

4. F, 5 _____

5. C, 2 _____

6. D, 0 _____

7. A, 1 _____

8. B, 3 _____

FS109039 • Math Activities

Roll 'Em

Mark the dice to match each problem, as shown. Then, find the product.

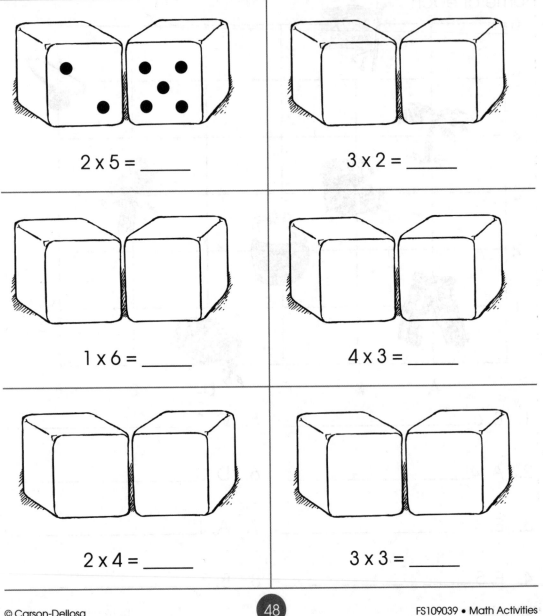

2 x 5 = _____

3 x 2 = _____

1 x 6 = _____

4 x 3 = _____

2 x 4 = _____

3 x 3 = _____

    FS109039 • Math Activities

Roller Skates

Write a multiplication problem to match each picture. Then, find the product.

____ X ____ = ____

____ X ____ = ____

____ X ____ = ____

____ X ____ = ____

FS109039 • Math Activities

Shape Up!

Multiply to find the answers. Color the shapes with even products **green** and those with odd products **purple**.

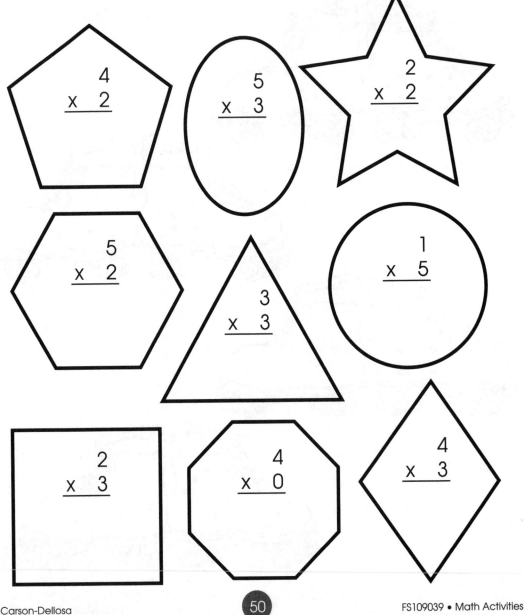

$$4 \times 2$$

$$5 \times 3$$

$$2 \times 2$$

$$5 \times 2$$

$$3 \times 3$$

$$1 \times 5$$

$$2 \times 3$$

$$4 \times 0$$

$$4 \times 3$$

FS109039 • Math Activities

Big Diamond

Find the products to crack the code and answer the riddle.

Where is the largest diamond in New York City kept?

$$\overline{2} \quad \overline{8} \qquad \overline{16} \quad \overline{0} \quad \overline{8} \quad \overline{10} \quad \overline{9} \quad \overline{9}$$

$$\overline{6} \quad \overline{4} \quad \overline{0} \quad \overline{3} \quad \overline{2} \quad \overline{5} \quad \overline{12}\,!$$

A	S	K
6 x 0	2 x 3	5 x 2
D 3 x 1	**I** 2 x 1	**R** 1 x 1
N 4 x 2	**T** 2 x 2	**Y** 4 x 4
M 2 x 6	**E** 3 x 3	**U** 1 x 5

DO NOT TOUCH

Page 2

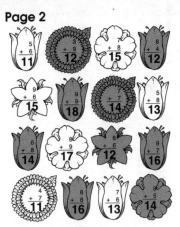

11, 12, 15, 12
15, 18, 14, 13
14, 17, 12, 16
11, 16, 13, 14

Page 3

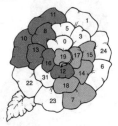

11, 10, 8, 13, 16, 12;
7, 18, 14, 15, 16, 17, 19
The ladybug should be circled.

Page 4

6, 7, 6; 4, 6, 6; 7, 7, 8

Page 5

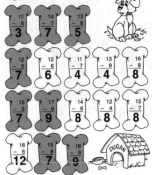

Page 6

23, 24, 40, 41, 19, 20
76, 77, 85, 86, 61, 62
97, 98, 39, 40, 92, 93
58, 59, 54, 55, 70, 71

91, 92, 46, 47, 19
32, 33, 80, 81, 69, 70
64, 65, 9, 10, 53, 54
85, 86, 97, 98, 78, 79

Page 7

Page 8

7 tens 3 ones, 70 + 3, 73;
6 tens 8 ones, 60 + 8, 68;
4 tens 9 ones, 40 + 9, 49;
5 tens 0 ones, 50 + 0, 50;
4 tens 7 ones, 40 + 7, 47;

Page 9

1. potatoes 2. peas 3. carrots 4. onions 5. corn 6. lettuce

Page 10

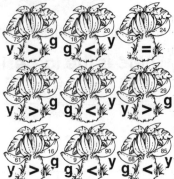

$y > g$ $g < y$ $=$
$y > g$ $g < y$ $y > g$
$y > g$ $g < y$ $g < y$

Page 11

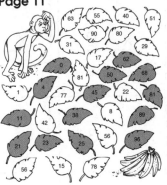

Page 12

3:00, 2:45, 5:30, 10:15

Page 13

1:20, 11:50; 6:35, 8:10

FS109039 • Math Activities

Page 14

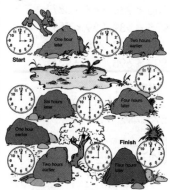

Page 15

Harry—6:40; Sue—2:20; Renee—1:45; Hannah—7:45; twins—12:25; Freddy—12:00

Page 16

35, 69, 98; 76, 99, 39; 79, 49, 91; 47, 86, 29; 97, 74, 56
The McCoys are the winners.

Page 17

Page 18

r 58 + 13 = **71**
y 23 + 17 = **40**
b 64 + 29 = **93**
p 15 + 15 = **30**

y 44 + 9 = **53**
b 57 + 37 = **94**
p 27 + 6 = **33**
r 46 + 28 = **74**

b 45 + 49 = **94**
p 18 + 19 = **37**
r 38 + 38 = **76**
y 36 + 16 = **52**

Page 19

AT THE BOTTOM
92, 83, 90, 61, 63; 94, 76, 35, 62, 91; 42, 54, 47, 70, 88

Page 20

71, 23, 21, 35, 22; 30, 34, 32, 73, 43; 51, 62, 59, 46, 68
The Fastbacks are the winners.

Page 21

72 = 7 tens and 2 ones = **6** tens and **12** ones

50 = 5 tens and 0 ones = **4** tens and **10** ones

23 = 2 tens and 3 ones = **1** tens and **13** ones

85 = 8 tens and 5 ones = **7** tens and **15** ones

90 = 9 tens and 0 ones = **8** tens and **10** ones

64 = 6 tens and 4 ones = **5** tens and **14** ones

Page 22

HE WAS HANGING BY HIS TEETH!
46, 19, 49, 9, 28; 67, 38, 35, 74, 52; 17, 63, 5, 25, 39

Page 23

96 − 25 = **71**
82 − 16 = **66**

− 18 = **53**
76 − 38 = **38**

− 29 = **24**
− 36 = **30**

− 18 = **6**
− 29 = **1**
− 29 = **9**
80 − 76 = **4**

6,194

Page 24

62, 80; 85, 97; 78, 63

Page 25

Answers will vary. The following are examples.

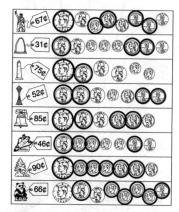

67¢
31¢
75¢
52¢
85¢
46¢
90¢
66¢

Page 26

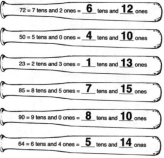

Anna bought a and a 🪱 How much did she spend altogether?	26¢ + 40¢ = **66¢**	Nick had 92¢ He bought a 🐭 How much did he have left?	92¢ − 73¢ = **19¢**
Stephen had 84¢ He bought a 🐛 How much does he have left?	84¢ − 38¢ = **46¢**	Rosie bought a and a 🐁 How much more did the 🐁 cost?	57¢ − 39¢ = **18¢**
Mitch bought two 🐻 How much did he spend in all?	47¢ + 47¢ = **94¢**	Lily bought a and a 🪱 How much more did the 🐱 cost?	40¢ − 26¢ = **14¢**

Page 27

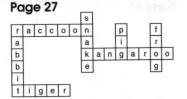

Across: 2. 47; 5. 73; 6. 57
Down: 1. 26; 2. 39; 3. 38; 4. 40

Page 28

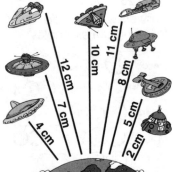

Page 29

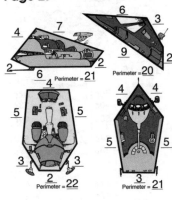

Perimeter = 21
Perimeter = 20
Perimeter = 22
Perimeter = 21

Page 30

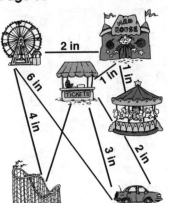

Page 31

1, 1, 1, 3, 6; 12 inches
3, 4, 2, 1, 3; 13 inches

Page 32

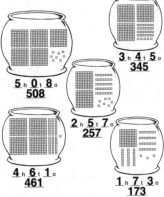

3 h 4 t 5 o
345

5 h 0 t 8 o
508

2 h 5 t 7 o
257

4 h 6 t 1 o
461

1 h 7 t 3 o
173

Page 33

1 h 4 t 5 o — $1.45
1 h 6 t 5 o — $1.65
1 h 6 t 3 o — $1.63
1 h 6 t 2 o — $1.62
2 h 3 t 1 o — $2.31
1 h 7 t 5 o — $1.75

Page 34

646 < 988, 867 > 687
975 < 989, 339 < 559
758 = 758, 295 > 289
893 > 698, 934 = 934

Page 35

774, 580, 591, 923, 960
575, 492, 910, 963, 794

Page 36

r 175 + 532 = 707
o 632 + 184 = 816
b 64 + 73 = 137
o 489 + 340 = 829
g 187 + 191 = 378
r 358 + 251 = 609
p 242 + 271 = 513
b 85 + 84 = 169
p 397 + 160 = 557
g 233 + 93 = 326
o 491 + 454 = 945
p 346 + 127 = 473

Page 37

FOR MAKING A EWE TURN!
681, 785, 913, 624, 565
936, 892, 577, 684, 782
712, 982, 470, 389, 333

Page 38

518 − 414 = 104	842 − 621 = 221	966 − 234 = 732	549 − 321 = 228
916 − 113 = 803	385 − 224 = 161	309 − 203 = 106	977 − 863 = 114
459 − 100 = 359	749 − 637 = 112	496 − 260 = 236	928 − 210 = 718
839 − 324 = 515	578 − 241 = 337	659 − 6 = 653	948 − 243 = 705

FS109039 • Math Activities

Page 39
405, 338, 229, 518
527, 554, 7, 207
119, 606, 429, 426

Page 40
Across: 1. 144;
3. 284; 4. 752;
6. 296; 8. 101;
9. 486; 10. 822

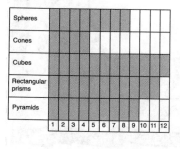

Down: 2. 422;
5. 592; 7. 690;
8. 168

Page 41
394, 491, 395, 438
91, 637, 383, 374
403, 502, 318, 464
Team B wins.

Page 42
Tara: $9.42 – $3.37 = $6.05;
$6.05 – $1.14 = $4.91
Kyle: $5.29 + $1.14 = $6.43;
$6.43 + $3.37 = $9.80

Page 43
$5.29 + $1.14 = $6.43;
$4.33 – $2.83 = $1.50;
$2.83 – $2.67 = $0.16, or 16¢;
$3.08 + $3.08 = $6.16;
$4.37 – $3.36 = $1.01;
$7.81 – $3.36 = $4.45

Page 44

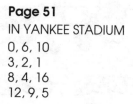

	1	2	3	4	5	6	7	8	9	10	11	12
Spheres												
Cones												
Cubes												
Rectangular prisms												
Pyramids												

Page 45
12 – 4 = 8; 9 + 8 = 17;
11 – 8 = 3; 4 + 11 + 12 = 27;
The cones; pyramids and spheres; 24

Page 46
1. B, 1; 2. D, 5; 3. E, 3; 4. C, 6;
5. A, 3; 6. D, 2; 7. C, 4; 8, F, 1

Page 47
Wording of answers may vary.
1. Flag 2. Palm tree
3. Parrot 4. Eye patch
5. Jug 6. Hat
7. Pants 8. Treasure chest

Page 48
Check drawings.
10, 6; 6, 12; 8, 9

Page 49
2 x 5 = 10; 6 x 1 = 6; 2 x 4 = 8;
3 x 3 = 9

Page 50

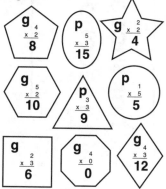

Page 51
IN YANKEE STADIUM
0, 6, 10
3, 2, 1
8, 4, 16
12, 9, 5

has successfully completed
this second-grade math book!

signature

date